THIS IS WHAT I

See

and

Hear

A Vision of Events to Come

JUDITH G. LINGENFELTER

CREATION HOUSE

THIS IS WHAT I SEE AND HEAR by Judith G. Lingenfelter
Published by Creation House
A Charisma Media Company
600 Rinehart Road
Lake Mary, Florida 32746
www.charismamedia.com

Unless otherwise noted, all Scripture quotations are from the King James Version of the Bible.

Scripture quotations marked AMP are from the Amplified Bible. Old Testament copyright © 1965, 1987 by the Zondervan Corporation. The Amplified New Testament copyright © 1954, 1958, 1987 by the Lockman Foundation. Used by permission.

Scripture quotations marked NKJV are from the New King James Version of the Bible. Copyright © 1979, 1980, 1982 by Thomas Nelson, Inc., publishers. Used by permission.

Direct quotes from the Lord are as He spoke to Judy about events, visions, and their meanings.

Artwork and illustrations were painted and drawn by Judith Lingenfelter.

Design Director: Bill Johnson
Cover design by Terry Clifton

Library of Congress Cataloging-in-Publication Data: 2013952184

International Standard Book Number: 978-1-62136-708-6
E-book International Standard Book Number: 978-1-62136-709-3

While the author has made every effort to provide accurate telephone numbers and Internet addresses at the time of publication, neither the publisher nor the author assumes any responsibility for errors or for changes that occur after publication.

First edition

14 15 16 17 18 — 9 8 7 6 5 4 3 2 1
Printed in the United States of America

DEDICATION AND THANKS

This book is dedicated to my grandchildren.

Thanks to Randy Hardy for photos of paintings.

ACKNOWLEDGMENT

THIS BOOK WAS compiled and edited by Pastor Wendy J. Schmeling, who is a great personal friend of mine and a visionary. While she has served the Lord since 1989, she was officially called into ministry in 2005 and is fully credentialed and ordained by both The national Assemblies of God and the local PenFlorida District, where she resides and currently ministers as a women's ministry pastor.

I have had the privilege of being her mentor as well as being a vital part of her ministry team. I have watched her put on amazing women's conferences, retreats, and fundraising functions for the women of the State of Florida. She is a dynamic preacher, teacher, speaker, and event planner. She is very talented and organized.

Wendy is called to a great ministry; a worldwide ministry that supports the vision of Isaiah 61. Jesus quoted this before He began His public ministry. Wendy's heart breaks for what breaks God's heart: the widow, the orphan, the poor, the girls and women who are trafficked into sexual slavery, the unborn, the mothers of aborted babies, and Muslim women—they are all very near and dear to God's heart, as well as Wendy's. I know Wendy is going to do great things for our Lord. I am looking forward to seeing her in action.

CONTENTS

PREFACE

I AM WRITING THIS book because there are many great and terrible things happening in our world today and in the days to come. These are things that cause people to wonder. These events cause people to worry, be afraid, and even lose hope.

The message the Lord has told me to share with you is this:

Impending judgment is coming!

Repent and return to the Lord.

God is good and His mercy endures forever.

My prayer and my hope is that in sharing what I have learned on my journey with God people will begin to see the big picture. While it may not look very encouraging at first glance, we are living in truly amazing and wondrous times. I hope to shed some light on what is happening so that people will not be afraid.

Many people question if there is a God; and if so, how can He let these things happen? I sincerely hope what I say in this book will answer some of those questions. One thing I do know is that God is love and He is for us and not against us (1 John 4:8, Rom. 8:31). While I may not know all of the answers to life's most serious questions, I know the One who holds the answers to it all. Please be encouraged as you read this book.

INTRODUCTION

Arise, shine; For your light has come! And the
glory of the LORD is risen upon you.

—ISAIAH 60:1, NKJV

AS WE TRAVEL the road in these end-time days, we are going to be amazed at the happenings that our God is bringing forth. We are living in the last days of this earthly age. The world is not coming to an end, but this season or age of the world is.

The Lord had a plan from the beginning for a perfect world. He created a perfect world with no disease, no pain, no death, no decay, no lack or want, and no sense of time. In the garden there was more than enough. There was an abundance of God's creation and blessings. Nothing was missing or broken. However, this all changed when the enemy, in the form of a serpent, slithered in. He convinced mankind (both Adam and Eve) to trade what they had, for what they thought they were missing. It was all based on a lie.

Unfortunately for us, Adam and Eve believed the lie. This is when sin came into the world and everything changed. This began the Earth Age, where perfection was traded for imperfection. Truth was replaced with lies. Life was replaced with death. Abundance was replaced with lack. In this earthly age we are caught up in a war between good and evil.

This was the reason Jesus had to come to earth. He had to restore what was corrupted. He began a restorative work when He came to this world, died on the cross, and was resurrected. However, that work is still not complete and will not be completed until the age that is yet to come. This is the Millennial Age, when Christ will rule and reign in a perfected world. A perfect world was always in His plans for mankind, whom He loves dearly. God is in the business of making all things new (Rev. 21:5). He is the God of second chances.

In His mercy and grace, God the Father has held off bringing a close to this age. He does this because He wills for not one person to perish without receiving the gift of redemption and salvation through His one and only Son, Jesus (2 Pet. 3:9). The time to choose Christ is now, in this age. The choice is always ours. God does not force us because He is a gentleman. He is a loving Father, not a cruel dictator. He waits patiently for mankind to realize that He truly is the only answer to our problems.

The King is coming! Jesus is coming to set up His kingdom— and soon. Once He comes, we will have 1,000 years of peace and prosperity. True believers are watching and waiting for this. This is not as good as it gets. There is a happy ending to this story. Greater things are yet to come!

When I asked Jesus into my heart and asked Him to be my Lord, many events took place in my life. This book is my journal of my walk with my Lord Jesus. Do not be afraid of what you read and see. There are a lot of things that our human minds simply cannot comprehend. God is more powerful, more beautiful, more pure and holy, more incredible than we can ever realize this side of heaven. His true attributes are far greater than we can handle. He is so holy that sin cannot enter into His presence. There is no darkness found in Him (1 John 1:5). He is the light of the world (John 8:12). If we looked at Him as He truly is we would be blinded by the intensity of His light.

God's ways are not our ways (Isa. 55:8). This is why some things related to God are hard for mankind to understand. We must always remember that God is good (Ps. 136:1), and He is always for us. He always loves us and wants the best for us.

Why is it that we will pay good money to go see science fiction movies that are far-fetched, but we can't stretch our minds to believe the glory and the wonder of our God? We have to rethink some things. I challenge you to do just that as you read this book. While I am sharing with you what God has shared with me, you should seek Him for yourself. Ask Him to open your eyes and show you what He wants to show you. Be open to Him.

THE ANGELS

Window to Heaven: The Journey

"SIMONEE, RECEIVE THE light of knowledge," were the words that awakened me early one morning. As I sat up in bed and looked toward the ceiling, I could see a spark of light. The light was high in the heavens, beyond the roof of my house. I continued to watch it, and the light grew bigger and brighter as it was coming closer and closer toward me. When the light touched me, it exploded into my heart. This was how I received the Holy Spirit. Now I didn't know this at the time. I didn't even know who the Holy Spirit was. However, now I do.

Going back to the month before this happened, I realized that there was a real God. As I knelt at the bottom of my bed and asked Jesus to come into my life and be my Lord, I was visited by six beautiful and brightly colored angels. It was strange to me at first because they didn't look like the angels that I had previously envisioned. I thought angels had wings, wore white robes, and floated in the air. These angels that I saw were brightly colored. They did not have wings. They held books in their hands.

They talked to me and said, "Everything you want to know about our Lord, you will find in the Bible and other Christian books." Then, they simply disappeared into the shining light which had surrounded them. I was so overwhelmed that I could not speak. I just sat on my bedroom floor for what seemed to be hours. How could such a thing happen? I had not picked up my Bible for thirty years, and I certainly didn't know what it said. This was the beginning of an amazing journey; a journey different than most, but here is my testimony.

At the time I asked Jesus into my heart and life, I was given the gift of discerning spirits, which I didn't know or understand until years later. I began having new and sometimes frightening experiences that I wasn't mentally or emotionally prepared for. The visions and dreams I started having were actually God communicating with me. You see, God wants us to understand what He is trying to show us or tell us. Sometimes it is too hard for us to grasp unless we see it. This is why often times the Lord communicates with us through dreams and visions.

I know that I was not going crazy when I began hearing awesome things. The "voices" I started hearing were very upsetting, yet fascinating. I began to read my Bible every day and researching everything that I had questions about.

The name "Simonee" was something I researched for about three months. I found the name in a little book of baby names in a Christian bookstore. "Simonee" means "one who hears." it also means "diligent" and "steadfast." Once I found the meaning of the name, I knew I wasn't crazy. God really does talk to people! All through the Bible we have examples of where

God revealed Himself to men. God wants to communicate with you too.

They say that a picture is worth a thousand words. Well, I have a lot to say. The Lord gave me a talent to paint pictures of my visions, and I have kept a journal of the many things the Lord has said. This book is a collection of my visions with revelations from the Lord as to the meanings. They have been kept for a time such as this. May the Lord bless and give you hope and peace in these last days.

For His Glory

God said the following things to me about His glory:

> You must tell the people this: God loves everyone. Call on the name of the Lord Jesus; repent, so that none should perish.

> Passover by the blood

> Don't worry or concern yourself with worldly things. The less you have on earth, the more you will have in heaven. Walk in truth and righteousness.

> Do the Great Commission.

> Firstfruits to the Father; Honor the Lord with your possessions and with the firstfruits of all your increase; so your barns will be filled with plenty.

> Now, stand on the promises of God, your Savior.

Chapter 2

THE CHRISTIAN WALK

PSALM 40:2 SAYS, "He brought me up also out of a horrible pit, out of the miry clay, and set my feet upon a rock, and established my goings." Once we accept Jesus and ask Him to come into our hearts, we start a journey that's wonderful and amazing. We are brought out of our old life, and a new life begins.

I painted "The Christian Walk" as the Lord showed it to me. There is much meaning to it, as well as symbolism. The rock represents the solid Rock, the Rock of Ages, or Jesus, who is the foundation. The cross is where everything begins. Jesus is the living sacrifice for our sins. The cross represents His death as a sacrifice for our sins. He is our salvation. The green grass represents the earth. The water coming from the rock represents the Holy Spirit, our helper and power to overcome.

The first step is to accept Jesus and move upward within our salvation. It is a process and a journey. It is not a onetime thing. It is not like punching your ticket to heaven and then living life as usual. The second step is to make Jesus our Lord. As the steps ascend, we move higher and higher on our journey and into deeper fellowship (our relationship with Jesus). As we move higher, we learn God's principles and experience His presence. We move up by building our faith and by prayer.

As you look at the painting, you will notice that the steps are not all the same. Some are rougher and wider than others. Some steps we must spend more time on, as we learn obedience, wisdom, or sanctification (holiness). Some steps are steps of praise, where we just give God thanks for who He is and what He has done or will do for us. The very last step is the image of Christ. This is where true perfection is.

Remember, the Christian walk is truly a process. None of us are perfect. We are all on a journey, and that is all right. Be faithful to the journey. Stay on course. Our goal is to reach that top step, where we are transformed into the image of the One and only One who was ever perfect.

God said the following things concerning the Christian walk:

The blood of Jesus is the living sacrifice for your sins.

He who the Son has set free is free indeed (John 8:36).

Jesus is the Resolute Protector.

Condemn no one.

Seek the kingdom of God first, and all things shall be added unto you (Matt. 6:33).

The wrath of God shall sit upon the enemy forever; the fire and the destroyer shall sit down together.

Ground yourself in the Word.

Be an empty bucket. Blessings flow in and blessings flow out to other people.

Be of good cheer; I have overcome the world (John 16:33).

Learn to lean on Jesus.

The Lord will make a way where there is no way.

Cross over the bridge of faith.

Yellow ribbons; happiness

Knife; crucifixion of fleshly desires

Abide in Me.

Chapter 3

THE HORSES

IN 1998 I had a vision of horses. This was an open vision. I looked up into the sky and saw six horses going around and around in a circle. They were magnificent! I watched them as they were twisting and turning, kicking and biting.

The Lord then told me He was putting down His heel (judgment) and nature is rebelling because of all of the evil on the earth. Here is the meaning of the vision. The horses stand for power and work. The six horses stand for mankind and the weakness of man and the manifestation of sin. The circle encompasses the world. The white horse stands for deception and falseness. Since there are three white horses, it means three times the power to deceive mankind.

> And Jesus answered and said unto them, "Take heed that no man deceive you."
>
> —MATTHEW 24:4

> And Jesus answering them began to say, "Take heed lest any man deceive you."
>
> —MARK 13:5

> Little children, let no man deceive you.
>
> —1 JOHN 3:7

The red horse takes peace from the earth in an act of war. The black horse stands for the economy, balance, famine, and disease and measures out justice. In Psalm 33:17 the horse also represents a type of human resource (power or government) in which people trust for their deliverance instead of the living God. There are only three colors in this vision because the next horse to come on the scene is the pale horse (death). Revelation 6:8 says that hell follows and one-fourth of the earth will be killed with sword, hunger, and with the beasts of the earth. This is yet to come, but the judgments have begun. These horses are here today working around the world.

God said the following things concerning this vision of "The Horses:"

> Put on therefore, as the elect of God, holy and beloved, bowels of mercies, kindness, humbleness of mind... and above all these things, put on charity [love], which is the bond of perfectness.
>
> —COLOSSIANS 3:12, 14

Love Me with all your heart

Chapter 4

THE HORSEMEN

IN 1998 I received another open vision. I looked up into the sky and saw horsemen galloping across the heavens. The sky was very dark behind them, and there was much rumbling and loud noises over the tree tops. The riders seemed to be wearing uniforms that were casual but identical.

The horsemen wore black slacks (pants) and black and gray striped shirts. They had black hair that looked almost like turbans. They were in formation, as an army riding together. However, they did not have a leader. These horsemen were riding forth to cover the earth as warhorses. The horses represent types of power and work. The garment represents the character of people (wicked, sinful in their manner of living). The black horse represents famine, wars, and disease. This is due to a lack of balance. Zachariah 6:1–6 speaks of horses released on the earth for judgment.

When I saw the vision, there was much noise among the horsemen. They rode as one unit with no leader. They were like a swarm of locusts. This painting is symbolic of the locust army going forth today. Joel 2:4–6 says,

> The appearance of them [locusts] is as the appearance of horses; and as horsemen, so shall they run. Like the noise of chariots on the tops of mountains shall they [locusts] leap, like the noise of a flame of fire that devoureth the stubble, as a strong people set in battle array. Before their face the people shall be much pained: all faces shall gather blackness [sorrow].

God said the following things concerning this vision of "The Horsemen:"

> When Jesus comes, the power of Satan is broken.

> Open your eyes to ministry.

> Moonlight serenade; reflect the light of Jesus with music.

> Be still and know that I am God (Ps. 46:10).

> Abide in me; words release power.

> Claim victory before the manifestation.

> Flying means overcoming and/or pressing in.

> Trust and obey.

> I am in control.

> The steps of the good man are ordered by the Lord; and He delights in his way (Ps. 37:23).

> Christ is the corner and foundation for all God's purposes.

> Walk strong; you will never walk alone.

> Honeycomb is the sweetness of God's Word.

Butterfly is new life.

A kiss is a sign of trust and affection; either good or bad, true or false.

The promises of God for deliverance in times of trouble will only work for those who believe.

Stand on the Word of Jesus.

I am putting down My heel in the earth.

Whatsoever you do, do it heartily, as to the Lord, and not unto men (Col. 3:23).

Roses, roses; love of Jesus

Trust in the Lord with all your heart, and lean not on your own understanding (Prov. 3:5).

Supplant. Pray to ask earnestly and humbly.

There is a fence around you for protection by God for a mission.

Those who walk in darkness, the Lord has sent them to you.

The King is coming.

Jesus is coming.

Ring of fire: earthquakes are coming at the ring of fire.

Fire: God's judgment

Chapter 5

THE DARKNESS

IN THE SAME way the horsemen and horse are coming forth today, there is a great darkness coming over the world. I have seen this darkness several times like a rolling cloud of blackness over cities, towns, and the countryside. Isaiah 60:2 says, "For, behold, the darkness shall cover the earth, and gross darkness the people." Gross here means thick or thickness. Darkness means sorrow, fear, deceit, misery, destruction, affliction, despair, rebellion, self-seeking, anxiety, wickedness, and confusion.

Joel 2:2 says, "A day of darkness and of gloominess, a day of clouds and of thick darkness." This darkness is controlled by the prince of darkness (Satan, the New World Order) trying to push God out and let men rule.

The only light here is the light of Jesus and the church. Darkness is the condition of the world just before the glory of the church shines forth. You are salt and light. People all over the world are in fear and searching for a safe place to live and hide their money as a way of protecting their family and homes. However, there is no guarantee of safety on earth except to abide in Jesus. He alone is able to deliver and will never forsake you (Heb. 13:5). He is faithful. Gross darkness is here. Don't be afraid because if it. Don't lose hope. You know Jesus overcame the darkness. Just be aware that it is here.

God said the following things concerning "The Darkness:"

Down the Mississippi to the Gulf of Mexico; I had a vision and I saw a *great* earthquake shaking the country and dividing the United States. The earthquake was in the center of the Mississippi River.

Judgment of the foundations

God's in control. It's just a matter of time.

Bells go on ringing for the beautiful and gracious testimony of God's people in service to the King.

Rain: precious blessings of God to receive and restore and refresh

The table of God makes provisions where there are no natural supplies.

The King is coming soon.

Lamplighter is the Word of Jesus.

Praise ye the Lord (Ps. 148:1). Sing unto the Lord a new song (Ps. 96:1).

One day at a time.

Be a messenger of peace.

Keep casting your fishing line. Keep throwing it into the waters.

Count your blessings.

Be like the ant and have high hopes.

Look to the stars now, see what is happening. The earth and the moon are giving up secrets. They are moving in a direction of completeness.

Babies being born today have a greater challenge in their life than ever before. Evil is running rampant. Protection for them is most important. Pray for the babies.

Watch the birds. Watch the sky. The clouds are gathering. The rains are coming. The floods are coming.

Civil war is coming to this country; brother against brother.

Mark the time.

Many changes are happening now.

Hold tight to what you have.

You will never walk alone.

Deception is flooding the world. Be diligent and disciplined.

Chapter 6

PSALM 91

Tʜɪs ɪs ᴀ great vision. The person represents any Christian man or woman. By faith we receive these words: "He who dwells in the secret place of the Most High Shall abide under the shadow of the Almighty" (Ps. 91:1, ɴᴋᴊᴠ). We must say or declare this out loud:

> I will say of the Lᴏʀᴅ, "He is my refuge and my fortress; My God, in Him I will trust." Surely He shall deliver [me] from the snare of the fowler And from the perilous pestilence. He shall cover [me] with His feathers, And under His wings [I] shall take refuge; His truth shall be [my] shield and buckler.
>
> —Psᴀʟᴍ 91:2–4, ɴᴋᴊᴠ

The shield is God's provision in the Messiah, who is our shield. This shield includes favor, salvation, truth, life, mercy, preservation, and security. The shield is also a covering. The circle is a circle of protection. The six-sided star is called the Shield of David or the star of the Jews. It means protection in the north, south, east, west, above, and below. A buckler is a coat of mail or armor. Armor is related to the circle in which one is surrounded. God's Word is your shield and armor (or weapon).

"[I] shall not be afraid of the terror by night [the darkness], Nor the arrow that flies by day" (v. 5, NKJV). The arrow represents something that pierces, severs, or wounds (this could be an accident, major illness, missiles, or bullets—anything that wounds you). In this painting, lightening represents arrows.

> Nor for the pestilence that walks in darkness [plagues or disease], Nor for the destruction [earthquakes, tornadoes, hurricanes, fire, floods, etc.] that lays waste at noonday. A thousand shall fall at [my] side, And ten thousand at [my] right hand; but it shall not come near me. Only with [my] eyes shall [I] look, And see the reward of the wicked. Because [I] have made the LORD, who is my refuge, Even the Most High, [my] dwelling place. No evil shall befall [me], Nor shall any plague come near [my] dwelling. For He [God] shall give His angels charge over [me], To keep [me] in all [my] ways.
> —PSALM 91:6–11, NKJV

"They [the angels] shall bear [me] up in their hands, lest [I] dash [my] foot against a stone. [I] shall tread upon the lion and adder: the young lion and the dragon shalt [I] trample under feet" (vv. 12–13). The lion represents dominion and strength to destroy. The young lion represents a destroying spirit that wants to devour you. The adder or snake represents devils, evil forces, darkness, traps, sorcery, and curses. The dragon represents Satan and the enemy. In this painting, the dragon (crocodile or alligator) represents evil of old and generational curses. It is a very destructive spirit.

Because I have set my love upon Him (God), therefore He will deliver me. He will set me on high, because I have known His name. I shall call upon Him, and He will answer me. He will be with me in trouble. He will deliver me, and honor me. With long life will He satisfy me, and show me His salvation (vv. 14–16).

There is so much in this painting that the Lord revealed to me. First, this is our position under God's wings. Your protection is to stay close to Him. All of the animals are symbols of the enemy. The bears are destroyers and stand for destruction, including financial loss.

Bulls represent persecution and opposition. Dogs represent confusion or harassment and take away your peace. Frogs represent unclean spirits and illness.

Bees represent biting words, gossip, and meanness to cause affliction. Scorpions represent lusts; lust of the eyes, flesh, and money. The scorpion's sting sends poison into your backbone and then rots the rest of the flesh.

Luke 10:19 says that we have the power to tread on serpents and scorpions. This means that we have power to trample on a curse, nullify it, and put down our sin nature or lust.

Pigs represent something unclean, a plague, and disease. Goats symbolize unbelief and takers; in this world there are takers and givers. Today God is separating the goat nations and the sheep nations. The leopard represents a demonic principality or spirit. Flies represent lies. The turkey is symbolic of being foolish.

Since the enemy's goal is to hurt us with so much destruction, the challenge is for us to stay under God's protective wing. So, how do we stay in position under God's wing? We do this through renewing our minds through the Word (reading our Bible) and obedience, obedience, obedience.

Chapter 7

NATURAL DISASTERS

AUGUST 10, 1998

I heard the Lord say, "Pray for San Francisco."

AUGUST 12, 1998

Today an earthquake hit San Francisco. Lots of property damage. I heard the Lord say the following in regard to this earthquake:

> Be watchful and keep your protection and wits about you.

> Fear not, for I am with you; be not dismayed; for I am your God (Isa. 41:10).

> Get busy and overcome.

AUGUST 24, 1998

I heard the Lord say, "Pray for Alabama."

SEPTEMBER 3, 1998

Hurricane Earl hit the coast of Alabama and North Florida with much flooding. The Lord had the following things to say regarding this storm:

> Kings and kingdoms will fall, but the word of Jesus will never fail.

> Be like the ant and have high hopes.

> Young at heart

> Through it all, Jesus will be there.

JANUARY 29, 1999

Pray for New Orleans.

Trust in the Lord.

There are only two kinds of people: saved and lost.

Be happy.

Don't be asleep on the battlefield.

Wake up.

Carry everything to God in prayer.

Chapter 8

9/11

September 11, 2001

June 21, 1999

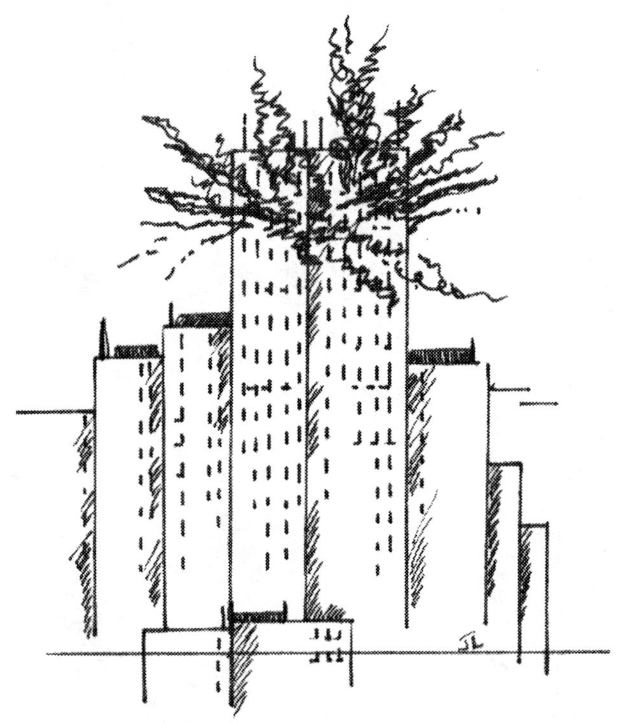

Vision:

Saw fire in high buildings
Explosions
High place of proud and power

THE LORD GAVE me a terrible vision. I saw fire in high buildings and an explosion. Of course, this was the terror attacks of September 11, 2001. While in the natural it was an attack of Muslim terrorists, in the spiritual realm it was an attack on the high places of power and pride in our nation. Unfortunately, there were innocent people caught in the middle of all of this. The Lord said much to me concerning this vision:

Life can never be exactly like you want it to be.

Put cares aside.

Jehovah-Jireh (my Provider)

There are two ministries—one in front and one in back. The important one is the back; the ministry that no one sees. It is a ministry of prayer and study of the Word.

Get the Bible inside you.

Little is much when God is in it.

God can fix any broken heart.

You are kept by a mighty strong hand.

Forgive everyone.

The gifts of the Spirit are for warfare.

Wisdom is the principle thing.

Hurting and broken hearts are my specialty for healing. Trust more.

Pray, read, and absorb more.

Praise and worship are ways to enter My gates.

Problems must be prayed over.

The earth is groaning for the Lord's return.
Be aware of mighty happenings in the world.

Be at peace. That is your victory.

Tests are all a part of life.

Praise

Go forward in laughter.

Encouragement to others is very important.

Praise and worship are the keys to everything.

Pray for revelation, knowledge, and wisdom.

Humbling yourself opens doors that nothing else can.

Worship produces My power and anointing.

Horses are galloping around the world right now and causing much harm and grief. [horses in the spiritual world represent power].

The sands of time are almost gone.

Pray for the people. Time is moving very fast now. Look to Me for guidance. Much work is to be done.

Read about My covenant with you.

Many things are happening around the world at this time. The earth is in travail awaiting its King. Wonders are unfolding. Keep watch.

Devils must flee at the name of Jesus.

Wisdom is the main thing.

Satan will be thrown from heaven soon, woe to the earth. Time is short.

Mercy will abound. Do not fear; the innocent will be protected.

This world is going to be shaken.

Many days of testing will take place.

Hope in Me. Never lose hope.

Keep trust. Keep close.

My world will be true and good, not counterfeit. Many a day I sorrow for the lost in this age. Help all you can. Those seeds will grow. Keep sowing them.

Don't lose heart.

Hope is not just a word but a state of being.

Have faith, hope, and charity [love]. My Word says it all.

Interpretation by Pastor Wendy Schmeling

The following is a literary insert in response to Judy's vision from June 21, 1999. This is a pastoral interpretation by Pastor Wendy J. Schmeling, ordained minister, with the Assemblies of God:

"What I believe the Lord was trying to say in regard to this attack on our great nation is that we can't make our lives what we want them to be and neglect others who are in need. We also have to make sure that our focus is not on ourselves or our own selfish gain. As a whole, our country has taken a turn for evil. We are no longer a nation who cares for the needs of others. We have become prideful and arrogant, thinking that we are higher and better than other nations. Greed has taken over our financial sector. America was not always like this. She was founded on biblical principles; and for almost a century lived, acted, and behaved based mostly on those principles.

Something began to change just prior the Civil War, and the change or shift increased with our progress as a nation to move into the twentieth century. The focus shifted off of God and His Word and onto productivity, growth, and industry. The race was on in the era of progress, and God was left out of the equation.

From that point in history up until now, as a nation we have been overcome and absorbed with progress, technology, doing things, and being busy. Technology was the new rave in the twenty-first century. I believe because man was successful with a few of his own ventures, he forgot who gave him the success and the know-how to do it in the first place.

The devil likes to distract us, make us busy, and keep us busy. If he can do this, if he can blind us to the real world of the spirit—the things that truly matter to God—then he has won half the battle. Our human nature kicks in and does the rest. It's hard work to live a dedicated life of prayer, fasting, studying the Word of God, fellowshipping with Him, and staying in His presence. All of this requires a relationship of intimacy, and relationships are hard work.

Now back to the vision and the events that took place on September 11, 2001. There has been a lot of spiritual misunderstanding concerning the terror attacks of 9/11. This is going to be hard for many to understand, but this event was allowed by God (I am speaking of the Christian God, not the Muslim God. They are not the same God). Please allow me to clarify something with the scriptures. In John 10:10, it is written that the thief (that's Satan) comes *only* to steal, kill, and destroy. This is his MO—modus operandi or mode of operation. This is how he has always been and always will be. You can expect these things from him, like clockwork or like the rising of the sun. So who is to blame for the 9/11 attacks? You guessed it. It's the devil. It's his MO.

There is another part of that scripture. It says, "But I [this is Jesus Christ himself speaking] came that [you] may have and enjoy *life*, and have it in abundance (to the full, till it overflows)" (John 10:10, AMP, emphasis added). So, even though the enemy comes to steal, kill, and destroy (remember, that's his MO, meaning he will *never* change or deviate from that plan), while that is how the devil works, Jesus is telling us how He always (without fail) works. God is love and God is life. He created life. He does not kill, steal, or destroy. We must, however, realize that we live in an imperfect world, which is rampant with sin.

Remember what happened in the Garden of Eden with Satan, who was then in the form of a slick, sly, and cunning serpent? He tricked Eve and indirectly Adam into thinking that God was keeping some things from them. He played on their sense of trust and curiosity. Remember his question to Eve? Has God really told you that? Did God really say that you could not eat from this one, little, insignificant, unimportant tree? Why would He tell you that? Didn't He create everything and declare that it was good? So then, what would be the harm in partaking in the goodness of His creation? Wouldn't you be honoring Him by taking a bite of this wonderful fruit that God Himself created? (See Genesis 3:1–5.) This is my interpretation of how that whole conversation went down. I took a little literary license to express what I think the devil was actually doing and saying to Eve.

Because we live in an evil world plagued with sin, because we know the devil only comes to kill, steal, and destroy, because we know that America as a whole has turned its back on God (the Christian God); in effect, we have kicked God out of many aspects of our lives. We kicked Him out of our schools with the removal of prayer and Bible reading in public schools in 1962. In 1973 the Supreme Court of our country made it legal for women to kill their unborn babies inside their wombs. Since then it is estimated that 50 million babies have been slaughtered, all in the name of "choice." Feminism and racism have plagued our nation and slapped God, who created us all to be equal, in the face. We kicked Him out of government halls and places of important decisions. Now we want Him off our money.

We as a nation have turned our backs on God. We as a nation have become prideful and self-sufficient, not needing God. The devil, who never stops his mission to kill, steal, and destroy, monopolized on this. You have to understand that God, unlike the devil, is a perfect gentleman. He leaves when we don't want Him. He does not overstay His welcome. The devil knows this. He also knows that our back turned on God is a covenant rule that cannot be broken or messed with. What I mean by this is that when God leaves, so does His hedge of protection. The only way to get it back is to invite God Himself back. So, knowing this, the devil swoops in for the kill.

We can't blame God for the terror attacks of 9/11 and say, "Where were You?" Remember, as a nation we told Him to leave. We said we didn't want Him. Then we take it a step further; in our grief and we yell at Him, shaking our fists, saying, "Why did You let this happen?" Remember, He cannot legally or rightfully protect us when we kick Him out of our life. He is a gentleman. When He goes, so goes His protection.

So, who is to blame for 9/11? First, and foremost, we are to blame. Anti-God America kicked God out; by this I mean an unrepentant nation kicked God out of all aspects of our daily lives.

Judgment is God's job alone. God Almighty (the Christian God) is slow to anger, rich in mercy, and quick to forgive (Ps. 145:8; Dan. 9:9). Yes, He is a God of justice (Isa. 30:18). Yes, He does judge us when we die, but He is love and He wills no one to perish and go to hell (1 John 4:8; 2 Pet. 3:9). He is all inclusive and wants everyone to accept His free gift of forgiveness through His only Son, Jesus Christ. For it is only in and through Him that we might be saved from God's judgment and wrath against sin.

Despite all of the evil that happened on 9/11, there were people repenting and crying out to God Almighty for help, protection, and forgiveness. The churches in America were packed in the hours, days, and months after the attacks. People were praying again. People were looking to God for answers. Unfortunately, this movement in the right direction did not last for long. After the sting of what happened wore off, many people went back to the status quo of business as usual; and God was forgotten again.

The sad thing is that many people don't see the cycle that keeps repeating itself like a skipping record. When we drift from God, who is our only lifeline and source of life itself, we doom ourselves. We are the ones that walk away from Him. He is very clear in His Word that He never leaves or forsakes us (Heb. 3:5). But we leave and forsake Him all of the time, and then we wonder where He went and why we are unprotected and why bad things happen to us. When will this truth click in our brains and lock in? When will we get it? When will we truly understand how it all works?

It's all about a relationship. If you break up with someone, you can't be mad when they don't call you or send you gifts anymore. You can't be upset when they don't call you on your birthday or take you out to a special dinner. Why do we expect different from God? It's simple. When we tell Him to leave, He leaves, and all of His benefits leave too."

Chapter 9

GREAT AND TERRIBLE VISIONS

VISION OF A LARGE WHITE HORSE RUNNING THROUGH THE SKY

IN THIS VISION the white horse represents deception. I also saw six soldiers lined up. Most of them were young and they were dressed in blue and gray uniforms. They had weapons. Some of the men were black and some of them were white. Then, I saw the words, "CIVIL WAR. Brother against brother. This is coming soon. Much turmoil."

I believe the Lord is saying that we are going to go through a time of great deception and will be faced with another civil war in this nation. The Lord also spoke to me concerning this vision. He had the following few things to say about it:

Walk the walk of faith. Be bold, love more. All is well.

Areas of obedience to My will are most important. Keep seeking.

Deception is flooding the world. Help where you can. Changes are coming.

You are in the army; the army of God. You can't let the enemy have a hold over you. Time to grow up.

Be watchful; don't lose what you have already gained. Bend to Me.

Jesus must be the center and light of all revelation. Everything was created for Jesus. Everything functions for Jesus. Jesus is the center of everything.

OLD TESTAMENT—JESUS—NEW TESTAMENT
THE BIBLE

Victory in Jesus, always

Testing will always be there as you grow. Everything changes. You are not alone. New things are a challenge.

New beginnings are always endings to other things.

Be more flexible. Bring Jesus into every situation.

Heaven will be worth it all.

Trust in Jesus. Everything is alright.

Love is most important.

Tests are a part of life.

Victory in Jesus

Many hearts are hurting today and need understanding.

Babies being born today have a greater challenge in their life than ever before. Evil is running rampant. Protection for them is most important. Pray for the babies.

Jerusalem is a seething pot waiting to boil. Many tests are coming their way.

Hope in Jesus.

Freedom, freedom is coming. Hold on. Many things are happening in the spirit world. Many things are breaking loose and being brought forth.

Doubt and disbelief are enemies of the soul.

Be diligent and steadfast.

Move mountains.

Building a relationship with Me is the most important thing. There are no shortcuts; discipline and trust.

Build good habits.

Move over to the Spirit's way of doing things:
Confession
Proclaiming
Moving mountains
Claiming
Spirit led

My will is always peace and joy.

Many are the trials of My children, but victory is always in the end—My way.

The problems of the nations all connected with idols and worship. Many are the afflicted due to lack of knowledge.

Guard yourself to the ways of evil.

True repentance is always from the heart. Mistakes are stepping stones for growth. Failure is only to not heed My voice.

There is a great awakening coming forth across this world. We must work together.

VISION OF A DARK SKY WITH MANY STARS AND THREE PLANETS BEHIND THE EARTH
NOVEMBER 6, 2000

I don't know what this means. Revelation will come.

Get stronger and be wiser.

Have a thankful heart.

Be the soldier I called.

Learn My ways.

Generations have been lost due to no foundation in My Word.

Build that road for the King is coming. The King is coming. Be at peace.

The horses of power and might are marching across the world. Changes are happening everywhere. Time is coming to a close. Jesus is coming back to earth soon. The accumulation of all things will be judged. Be aware of changes and seasons. March forward. The light must be carried forward. Major happenings will occur. Be at peace—My peace.

Man shall not break My laws and not reap wrath.

Mercy and grace shall abound, but I will not be mocked.

Strength is not in your own ability but trusting Me.

All of My children need guidance. Some are easier than others to bend. I love you.

God, the poet:
  Bees make honey.
  Birds make songs.
  Love makes children for God.

Tomorrow many things will come forth; be not dismayed.

Tell the story of the Cross to everyone.

The light that goes forth will surely shine. The way will clear.

Many are the tricks of the enemy. The night is coming soon. You must be sharp.

Some day the earth will move to and fro to the beat of evil drummers.

Truly, this is the time of obedience and labor of love.

The toll of disobedience is strong and effective.

Truly, I say, the bear [destroyer] and the fire [destruction] will set down together.

March forward with no fear; no looking behind.

The best is yet to come.

Gird up your loins and be tough.

Don't let the small things get to you.

My word will do all; My word is complete. Walk in sunshine today.

I knew you before this world age and your soul was created by Me.

You will project My glory because of love.

Rejoice. Let the past go.

Be still and know that I am God (Ps. 46:10).

Walk worthy of the Lord in all you do.

Put on the armor of God in these times and watch. Nations will rage for lack of understanding and end times will come upon them as a thief.

Surely, goodness and mercy shall follow you all the days of your life (Ps. 23:6). Worship!

Be all you can be. Lots of challenges

The table of showbread is the sustaining table before the Lord in the church; the days of old—of tradition and reverence of My priesthood and ways. Communion is a tradition to remind you of the great sacrifice Jesus made for you. And glory to Him. The oral tradition and confession and communion are being set aside. Bending of My Word is happening everywhere. Many are the griefs of My heart toward the falling away.

Men search everywhere for visions and miracles instead of Me. Knowing Me makes everything come into play. Peace be unto you.

Time is short. The King is coming and people aren't ready.

Testing will be strong. They must know My words.

Take the tough job of weeding out negative things and put aside. Take the story of David's first wife and learn from it. Resentment has no place. Walk strong and in love. Be diligent.

Pray for truth to come forth.

Rejoice.

Don't rely on men for knowledge or holding you up. The foundation work is yours to do.

Repent. Walk in the light.

Time is so precious. Jesus is coming back soon.

Wisdom is accepting your future with Me; dedication to pray, study, and work.

True worship is humbling oneself to Me in everything.

All the hosts of heaven are on alert for battle. Revival. The marriage supper is being prepared. Praise.

Rejoice, I have overcome the world (John 16:33).

The toll of disobedience is always sorrow.

The earth is in labor and the pains are coming closer and closer. The fall of nations is coming. Many will turn toward Me.

My joy is your strength (Neh. 8:10). Strength is leaning on Me.

Pursue the study of love.

Merry hearts heal.

It is time for true worship.

The making of a soldier is discipline.

The hearts of people must change.

Marchers are coming forth to destroy the peace and comfort of many.

The toll of disobedience will be heavy. This country will mark this day and remember days of old. Hold onto righteousness.

The top of the tower of Babel is coming down.

This is not a time of fear or rebellion but of trust and reflection, thanksgiving and rest in the Lord.

Changes are coming to everyone; every life will see change.

My will be done.

There is peace for everyone who looks to Me.

The war on evil is never ending while in this age. The sun will rise on a new age and this time will be forgotten. The people of a new beginning ordained of the Lord.

Be of good cheer, I have overcome the world (John 16:33).

Tell the old story of love.

Worship is a lifestyle of enjoying God.

Have patience for each person who is searching to find their way in the maze of life. This is not the time for self-indulgence.

Endeavor to persevere. Everyone is in a season of war. Find strength in Me.

The order of events is already in place. Twists and turns are coming near. Be sure your head is covered.

VISION OF LARGE ARMY MARCHING FOR WAR

I saw a large army marching or war. The Lord said the following concerning this vision:

There are 17 million.

Note the total of weapons marching on Israel. Now is the time for intercession.

Sometimes you can't see through the fog, but a blaze of My glory will cut through all problems. Fear not.

VISION OF MANY TORNADOS ACROSS THE UNITED STATES
OCTOBER 31, 2006

I saw a vision of a black sky. There were many tornados and many towns were destroyed. The Lord said the following to me about this terrible vision:

The day is dawning for relationships and love. Be all you can be.

All is well.

Nothing is too big for your God.

Call on Me and I will show you mighty things.

Acknowledge Me in everything.

The Port of New Orleans is gone. Repentance did not come.

This country is in shambles; pray more.

Great change is coming.

The conclusion of all things will depend upon repentance.

The harvest is ready.

The hearts of men are being robbed of peace.

Welcome combat; you win.

The enemy is very busy. Twin towers again; Hartford, CT. Pray.

Many hearts are being softened to hear God's words.

Walk the walk, talk the talk.

Trust Me.

Vision of the Freedom Tower
January 6, 2012

I saw the terrible destruction of the new Freedom Tower in New York City. At the time of this book, it is not even completed. When? I do not know.

This is a great burden to me. I take all of these happenings very seriously. My heart hurts for people. Years ago, when the Lord called me as a prophet to the nations with the "Jeremiah anointing," I could not even imagine the intense visions and happenings I have been involved in.

The One World Trade Center or Freedom Tower is very open to attack because God is not in it.

This is what the Lord told me:

Terrible things are coming forth; desperate times. Crime will increase. The ditch of wickedness is filling up.

Pray and repent.

The greatest revival is coming but also the greatest time of testing; trust and reflection. Cry out to God now for forgiveness and protection.

"Return to Me, and I will return to you," says the LORD of hosts.

—MALACHI 3:7, NKJV

THE TOWER OF BABEL

This represents the world system and the One World Trade Center (Freedom Tower).

And all the people shall know...that say in the pride and stoutness of heart, The bricks are fallen down but *we* will build with hewn stones: the sycamores are cut down, but *we* will change them into cedars.

—ISAIAH 9:9–10, EMPHASIS ADDED

Who have said, with our tongue will we prevail; our lips are *our* own: who is lord over *us*? For the oppression of the poor, for the sighing of the needy. Now will I arise, sayeth the Lord.

—PSALM 12:4–5, EMPHASIS ADDED

And they [nations] said, Go to, let *us* build *us* a city and a tower, whose top may reach unto heaven; and let *us* make *us* a name.

—GENESIS 11:4, EMPHASIS ADDED

The Lord also told me the following things:

Many people are wondering and hoping in other men. Spirits have taken over their minds. The will to become great in their own eyes is ever before them.

Humble yourselves and pray to me. My arm is not shortened that it cannot save (Isa. 59:1). My hand is stretched out still (9:21).

If the nation repents, there will be restoration of all things.

Chapter 10

THE GULF

I AWOKE EARLY ONE morning and felt the presence of the Lord all over me. I was transported, with angels on all sides of me, to some place high so I could see this great wide gulf, the dividing chasm between paradise and the edge of hell.

Luke 16:22–26 speaks about Jesus teaching about Lazarus and the rich man. They each went to a different place when they died. Between them was this great gulf, fixed and established, so that no one could pass over to either side.

This is paradise, a beautiful place of peace and love. All of the great men and women of the Bible and Christian saints of all generations are there.

I enjoyed watching what was happening there with the great colors and joyful atmosphere.

If you have any dear Christian relative or friends that have passed on, this is where they are. Have no fear. All babies and children that have gone on to be with the Lord are there.

The Lord let me see only a small part, but it is a wonderful place of love and learning. We can go back to my first painting, "The Christian Walk," with the steps going up. What you don't learn here on Earth, you will learn there; principles, obedience, praise, worship, rejoicing, etc.

Many people believe they are going to heaven to float around on a cloud and do nothing. Well, wake up! Your final destiny is to be like Jesus, so there is a lot of learning to do. I could see men and women looking as if they were teaching. Some appeared to be Old Testament saints, but I wasn't told who they were. I do know that Father Abraham is there. Jesus was there but I didn't see Him.

Paradise is a real place.

Hell is a real place.

These are holding places until judgment time—the great white throne judgment (Rev. 20:11).

Hell: I saw just the outer rim or ridge of the top of a large pit. It was foul smelling with oppressive heat. I could actually feel it. There was moaning and torment, a place of regret. I had a knowing that if I looked down I would see horrible things.

Because God has opened my eyes, I have seen demons as well as angels. However, I do not wish to scare you so I will not go into further detail of what the Lord showed me. I believe that the Lord gives visions and dreams to many; but He is also a gentleman so He does not show everyone everything, especially if they are not prepared to deal with it.

Chapter 11

THE THRONE ROOM

IN 1999, ON Christmas Eve, before sleeping, I asked the Lord if I could hear the angels sing. I felt I would really like that for a Christmas present. When was the last time you got out of your comfort zone and asked the Lord for something outrageous? Well, I got more that I asked for that night.

The glory came down and I was transported to the throne room of God. I heard the angels sing. There were thousands and thousands of angels singing. They were singing:

Hark, the herald angels sing, glory to the newborn King.

Wow! There is no more I can say, except it was hard to paint the bright dazzling light. I was so humbled. It was a Christmas I'll never forget.

Jeremiah 33:3 declares, "Call to Me, and I will answer you, and show you great and mighty things, which you do not know" (NKJV).

Chapter 12

THE HOLY CITY

ONE NIGHT THE Lord's glory came to me, and I was transported into a room that looked glorious with gold walls. I turned around and looked at beauty beyond anything I have ever seen. I was in a room that just shimmered. It was a library. I didn't want to touch anything because it all looked too elegant. As I turned around, I asked, "What is this, Lord?"

Instantly, I was pulled back and away to a mountaintop. On either side was an angel with wings. I looked and saw the Holy City. And the angels spoke, "Behold the Holy City; the New Jerusalem!"

The city seemed to be moving down out of heaven. It was surrounded by a clear greenish-blue glass. What a breathtaking sight!

This is not the millennium city of Jerusalem which is

described in Isaiah 65 and Ezekiel 40–48. That city is to be built and restored with King Jesus on the throne for 1,000 years.

This New Jerusalem is already there, above, and is described in Revelation 21 by the apostle John:

> And I John saw the holy city, the new Jerusalem, coming down from God out of heaven, prepared as a bride adorned for her husband....And he that sat upon the throne said, Behold I make all things new....And had a wall great and high, and had twelve gates, and at the gates twelve angels, and names written thereon, which are the names of the twelve tribes of the children of Israel: On the east three gates; on the north three gates; on the south three gates; and on the west three gates. And the wall of the city had twelve foundations, and in them the names of the twelve apostles of the Lamb....And the foundations of the wall of the city were garnished with all manner of precious stones.... And the twelve gates were twelve pearls: every several gate was of one pearl: and the street of the city was pure gold, as it were transparent glass.
>
> —REVELATION 21: 2, 5, 12–14, 19, 21

As I looked at the city, I thought about the library that was within. Why a library? That is where books are held. The Book of Life is there.

Revelation 20:11–13 talks about the books being opened. The great and the small will stand before God in the great white throne judgment, and everyone will be judged according to their works.

CONCLUSION

Wow! I have been so blessed to have such an amazing journey. But you have your own journey to make. Your choice to accept Jesus while you are on this earth will determine where you will spend eternity.

I have seen some wonderful things. I have been to some beautiful places. But the most beautiful thing to God is one soul who repents and comes to Jesus.

Are you sure you know where you are going when you die?

This is a message of *hope*, not of gloom and doom. Are we prepared for the returning of Jesus? He is coming back sooner that we think.

Now is the time to commit or recommit your life to Jesus. In the days to come, you will need to walk very close to your Lord.

Pray this prayer with me:

> *Lord Jesus, I repent of all my sins. Come into my life and make me new. I make You Lord of my Life. I give my heart to You. In Your name I pray. Amen.*

Finally, I leave you with one last word from the Lord Himself:

Love makes all things right.

ABOUT the AUTHOR

J UDITH G. LINGENFELTER was born in Niagara Falls, New York. She was raised in Pennsylvania. She married her high school sweetheart, Richard, and they have been married for fifty-one years. They have two daughters; Noel Wynn and Holly Carter. Judy and her husband have four grandsons; Nevada, Jackson, Zane, and Wyatt. They have lived in Florida for twenty-seven years. Judy and her family have been farmers for many years, raising beef cattle and growing citrus. Judy's one goal in life is to walk closely with God.

CONTACT the AUTHOR

JudithgLingenfelter@gmail.com

Judith G. Lingenfelter
P.O. Box 133
Lake Alfred, FL 33850